foreword by
Emilie Barnes

HARVEST HOUSE PUBLISHERS
Eugene, Oregon 97402

MY PRAYER PLANNER

Copyright © 1991 by Harvest House Publishers
Eugene, Oregon 97402

Library of Congress Cataloging-in-Publication Data

Barnes, Emilie.
    My prayer planner   /   by Emilie Barnes.
    ISBN 0-89081-875-4
    1. Prayer—Christianity.   I. Title.
BV215.B35   1991
248.3'2—dc20   90-23716
                                                          CIP

Printed in the United States of America.

How To Use
MY PRAYER PLANNER

My mind and my body may grow weak, but God is my strength; he is all I ever need (Psalm 73:26 TEV).

My Prayer Planner grew from a need in my own life during a time when I had five children under five years old. Proverbs 16:3 says we are to ask the Lord to bless our plans and we will be successful in carrying them out. My time was limited, but I made an appointment with God early every morning during which I committed my works as a wife, mother, and homemaker to Him. That's when I organized my daily prayer planner. Today as an author and speaker, traveling across country and back, running a home and, with my Bob, a "More Hours In My Day" ministry, I need more than ever to commit my days to the Lord.

Your prayer planner is already organized for you. Simply make a list of all your prayer requests. Then put them into topics and distribute these behind each day of the week in your planner. For example:

Monday—<u>Family</u>: Bob
Brad/Maria
Jenny/Craig
Christine/Caade/Bevan
Tuesday—<u>Illnesses</u>
Wednesday—<u>Church, Pastor</u>
<u>Missions</u>
<u>Ministries, etc.</u>

Each week you will cover every prayer need on your list and not be overwhelmed by 50 requests each day.

The box at the bottom is for a Scripture that could apply to the person you are praying for or a verse that stood out as you read your Bible. The box at the top of each page is for photos of those people you are praying for.

I have in my prayer planner a single page for each of our immediate family. On each grandchild's page I put a small photo (head shot) and draw an outline of their hand on the page. I draw a heart in the middle of their palm. As I pray for them I look at the picture and hold my hand over theirs. we may be miles apart, but as I pray our hearts beat together. I pray that each child will grow to love our Lord, serve Him, and walk in His steps.

Your prayer planner will become very close and special to your heart and prayer time. Date your requests and record the answers. God's timing is always perfect.

At the back you will find a place for significant thoughts, verses, or notes that come out of your time of prayer.

When our minds and bodies grow weak, let's keep in mind that God truly is our strength—His strength comes as we read His Word and communicate with Him in daily prayer. May your blessings be great.

Joyfully,

Emilie Barnes

Emilie

Sunday

It is helpful to ask ourselves as we pray, "Do I really expect anything to happen?" This will prevent us from going window-shopping in prayer. At times window-shopping can be enjoyable— but there it ends. It costs nothing…we bring home nothing to show for our hours of browsing.

Catherine Marshall

M Y • P R A Y E R • P L A N N E R

Photo or Other Visual Reminder

Prayer Request   *Date*

_____
_____
_____
_____
_____
_____
_____

Answer to Prayer   *Date*

_____
_____
_____
_____
_____
_____
_____

*P*rayer Verse _____
_____
_____
_____

M Y • P R A Y E R • P L A N N E R

Photo or Other Visual Reminder

Prayer Request   *Date*

_____

_____

_____

_____

_____

_____

_____

_____

Answer to Prayer   *Date*

_____

_____

_____

_____

_____

_____

_____

_____

*P*rayer Verse _____

_____

_____

_____

MY • PRAYER • PLANNER

Photo or Other Visual Reminder

Prayer Request   *Date*

_____

_____

_____

_____

_____

_____

_____

Answer to Prayer   *Date*

_____

_____

_____

_____

_____

_____

_____

Prayer Verse _____

_____

_____

_____

M Y • P R A Y E R • P L A N N E R

Photo or Other Visual Reminder

Prayer Request   *Date*

_____

_____

_____

_____

_____

_____

_____

Answer to Prayer   *Date*

_____

_____

_____

_____

_____

_____

_____

*P*rayer Verse _____

_____

_____

M Y • P R A Y E R • P L A N N E R

Photo or Other Visual Reminder

Prayer Request   *Date*

_____

_____

_____

_____

_____

_____

_____

Answer to Prayer   *Date*

_____

_____

_____

_____

_____

_____

_____

*P*rayer Verse _____

_____

_____

_____

MY • PRAYER • PLANNER

Photo or Other Visual Reminder

Prayer Request   *Date*

_____
_____
_____
_____
_____
_____
_____

Answer to Prayer   *Date*

_____
_____
_____
_____
_____
_____
_____

Prayer Verse _____
_____
_____
_____

M Y • P R A Y E R • P L A N N E R

Photo or Other Visual Reminder

Prayer Request   *Date*

_____
_____
_____
_____
_____
_____
_____

Answer to Prayer   *Date*

_____
_____
_____
_____
_____
_____
_____

*P*rayer Verse _____
_____
_____
_____

M Y • P R A Y E R • P L A N N E R

Photo or Other Visual Reminder

Prayer Request   *Date*

_____

_____

_____

_____

_____

_____

_____

Answer to Prayer   *Date*

_____

_____

_____

_____

_____

_____

_____

*P*rayer Verse _____

_____

_____

_____

M Y • P R A Y E R • P L A N N E R

Photo or Other Visual Reminder

Prayer Request   *Date*

_____

_____

_____

_____

_____

_____

_____

_____

Answer to Prayer   *Date*

_____

_____

_____

_____

_____

_____

_____

_____

*P*rayer Verse _____

_____

_____

_____

M Y • P R A Y E R • P L A N N E R

Photo or Other Visual Reminder

Prayer Request   *Date*

_____

_____

_____

_____

_____

_____

_____

Answer to Prayer   *Date*

_____

_____

_____

_____

_____

_____

_____

*P*rayer Verse _____

_____

_____

MY • PRAYER • PLANNER

Photo or Other Visual Reminder

Prayer Request   *Date*

_____
_____
_____
_____
_____
_____
_____

Answer to Prayer   *Date*

_____
_____
_____
_____
_____
_____
_____

*P*rayer Verse _____
_____
_____
_____

M Y • P R A Y E R • P L A N N E R

Photo or Other Visual Reminder

Prayer Request   *Date*

_____

_____

_____

_____

_____

_____

_____

Answer to Prayer   *Date*

_____

_____

_____

_____

_____

_____

_____

*P*rayer Verse _____

_____

_____

_____

M Y • P R A Y E R • P L A N N E R

Photo or Other Visual Reminder

Prayer Request   *Date*

_____
_____
_____
_____
_____
_____
_____

Answer to Prayer   *Date*

_____
_____
_____
_____
_____
_____
_____

*P*rayer Verse _____
_____
_____
_____

M Y • P R A Y E R • P L A N N E R

Photo or Other Visual Reminder

Prayer Request   *Date*

_____

_____

_____

_____

_____

_____

_____

Answer to Prayer   *Date*

_____

_____

_____

_____

_____

_____

_____

*P*rayer Verse _____

_____

_____

_____

<u>Monday</u>

*None can believe how
powerful prayer is, and
what it is able to effect,
but those who have
learned it by experience.*

Martin Luther

M Y • P R A Y E R • P L A N N E R

Photo or Other Visual Reminder

Prayer Request   *Date*

_____

_____

_____

_____

_____

_____

_____

Answer to Prayer   *Date*

_____

_____

_____

_____

_____

_____

_____

*P*rayer Verse _____

_____

_____

_____

M Y • P R A Y E R • P L A N N E R

Photo or Other Visual Reminder

Prayer Request   *Date*

_____

_____

_____

_____

_____

_____

_____

Answer to Prayer   *Date*

_____

_____

_____

_____

_____

_____

_____

*P*rayer Verse _____

_____

_____

_____

M Y • P R A Y E R • P L A N N E R

Photo or Other Visual Reminder

Prayer Request   *Date*

_____
_____
_____
_____
_____
_____
_____

Answer to Prayer   *Date*

_____
_____
_____
_____
_____
_____
_____

*P*rayer Verse _____
_____
_____
_____

M Y • P R A Y E R • P L A N N E R

Photo or Other Visual Reminder

Prayer Request   *Date*

_____

_____

_____

_____

_____

_____

_____

Answer to Prayer   *Date*

_____

_____

_____

_____

_____

_____

_____

*P*rayer Verse _____

_____

_____

_____

M Y • P R A Y E R • P L A N N E R

Photo or Other Visual Reminder

Prayer Request   *Date*

_____
_____
_____
_____
_____
_____
_____

Answer to Prayer   *Date*

_____
_____
_____
_____
_____
_____
_____

*P*rayer Verse _____
_____
_____
_____

M Y • P R A Y E R • P L A N N E R

Photo or Other Visual Reminder

Prayer Request   *Date*

_____

_____

_____

_____

_____

_____

_____

Answer to Prayer   *Date*

_____

_____

_____

_____

_____

_____

_____

*P*rayer Verse _____

_____

_____

_____

M Y • P R A Y E R • P L A N N E R

Photo or Other Visual Reminder

Prayer Request   *Date*

_____

_____

_____

_____

_____

_____

_____

Answer to Prayer   *Date*

_____

_____

_____

_____

_____

_____

_____

Prayer Verse _____

_____

_____

_____

M Y • P R A Y E R • P L A N N E R

Photo or Other Visual Reminder

Prayer Request   *Date*

_____

_____

_____

_____

_____

_____

_____

_____

Answer to Prayer   *Date*

_____

_____

_____

_____

_____

_____

_____

_____

*P*rayer Verse _____

_____

_____

_____

M Y • P R A Y E R • P L A N N E R

Photo or Other Visual Reminder

Prayer Request   *Date*

_____

_____

_____

_____

_____

_____

_____

Answer to Prayer   *Date*

_____

_____

_____

_____

_____

_____

_____

*P*rayer Verse _____

_____

_____

_____

M Y • P R A Y E R • P L A N N E R

Photo or Other Visual Reminder

Prayer Request   *Date*

_____

_____

_____

_____

_____

_____

_____

Answer to Prayer   *Date*

_____

_____

_____

_____

_____

_____

_____

Prayer Verse _____

_____

_____

_____

MY • PRAYER • PLANNER

Photo or Other Visual Reminder

Prayer Request   *Date*

_____

_____

_____

_____

_____

_____

_____

Answer to Prayer   *Date*

_____

_____

_____

_____

_____

_____

_____

Prayer Verse _____

_____

_____

_____

M Y • P R A Y E R • P L A N N E R

Photo or Other Visual Reminder

Prayer Request   *Date*

_____

_____

_____

_____

_____

_____

_____

Answer to Prayer   *Date*

_____

_____

_____

_____

_____

_____

_____

*P*rayer Verse _____

_____

_____

_____

M Y • P R A Y E R • P L A N N E R

Photo or Other Visual Reminder

Prayer Request   *Date*

_____

_____

_____

_____

_____

_____

_____

Answer to Prayer   *Date*

_____

_____

_____

_____

_____

_____

_____

*P*rayer Verse _____

_____

_____

_____

M Y • P R A Y E R • P L A N N E R

Photo or Other Visual Reminder

Prayer Request   *Date*

_____

_____

_____

_____

_____

_____

_____

Answer to Prayer   *Date*

_____

_____

_____

_____

_____

_____

_____

*P*rayer Verse _____

_____

_____

_____

Tuesday

*God expects us to be
orderly, He expects us
to manage our time,
to discipline ourselves,
to prepare well-planned pro-
grams, but if we could learn
to pray first and plan
afterward, how different
would be ...whatever we are
doing for Christ.*

Evelyn Christenson

M Y • P R A Y E R • P L A N N E R

Photo or Other Visual Reminder

Prayer Request *Date*

_____
_____
_____
_____
_____
_____
_____

Answer to Prayer *Date*

_____
_____
_____
_____
_____
_____
_____

*P*rayer Verse _____
_____
_____
_____

M Y • P R A Y E R • P L A N N E R

Photo or Other Visual Reminder

Prayer Request   *Date*

_____

_____

_____

_____

_____

_____

_____

Answer to Prayer   *Date*

_____

_____

_____

_____

_____

_____

_____

Prayer Verse _____

_____

_____

_____

M Y • P R A Y E R • P L A N N E R

Photo or Other Visual Reminder

Prayer Request   *Date*

_____
_____
_____
_____
_____
_____
_____

Answer to Prayer   *Date*

_____
_____
_____
_____
_____
_____
_____
_____

*P*rayer Verse _____
_____
_____
_____

MY • PRAYER • PLANNER

Photo or Other Visual Reminder

Prayer Request   *Date*

_____

_____

_____

_____

_____

_____

_____

Answer to Prayer   *Date*

_____

_____

_____

_____

_____

_____

_____

*P*rayer Verse _____

_____

_____

_____

MY · PRAYER · PLANNER

Photo or Other Visual Reminder

Prayer Request   *Date*

_____

_____

_____

_____

_____

_____

_____

Answer to Prayer   *Date*

_____

_____

_____

_____

_____

_____

_____

*P*rayer Verse _____

_____

_____

_____

M Y • P R A Y E R • P L A N N E R

Photo or Other Visual Reminder

Prayer Request   *Date*

_____

_____

_____

_____

_____

_____

_____

Answer to Prayer   *Date*

_____

_____

_____

_____

_____

_____

_____

*P*rayer Verse _____

_____

_____

_____

M Y • P R A Y E R • P L A N N E R

Photo or Other Visual Reminder

Prayer Request   *Date*

_____

_____

_____

_____

_____

_____

_____

Answer to Prayer   *Date*

_____

_____

_____

_____

_____

_____

_____

Prayer Verse _____

_____

_____

_____

Photo or Other Visual Reminder

Prayer Request   *Date*

_____

_____

_____

_____

_____

_____

_____

Answer to Prayer   *Date*

_____

_____

_____

_____

_____

_____

_____

*P*rayer Verse _____

_____

_____

_____

MY • PRAYER • PLANNER

Photo or Other Visual Reminder

Prayer Request   *Date*

_____
_____
_____
_____
_____
_____
_____

Answer to Prayer   *Date*

_____
_____
_____
_____
_____
_____
_____

*P*rayer Verse _____
_____
_____
_____

Photo or Other Visual Reminder

Prayer Request   *Date*

_____
_____
_____
_____
_____
_____
_____

Answer to Prayer   *Date*

_____
_____
_____
_____
_____
_____
_____

*P*rayer Verse _____
_____
_____
_____

M Y • P R A Y E R • P L A N N E R

Photo or Other Visual Reminder

Prayer Request   *Date*

_____
_____
_____
_____
_____
_____
_____

Answer to Prayer   *Date*

_____
_____
_____
_____
_____
_____
_____

*P*rayer Verse _____
_____
_____
_____

M Y • P R A Y E R • P L A N N E R

Photo or Other Visual Reminder

Prayer Request   *Date*

_____

_____

_____

_____

_____

_____

_____

Answer to Prayer   *Date*

_____

_____

_____

_____

_____

_____

_____

*P*rayer Verse _____

_____

_____

_____

M Y • P R A Y E R • P L A N N E R

Photo or Other Visual Reminder

Prayer Request   *Date*

_____
_____
_____
_____
_____
_____
_____

Answer to Prayer   *Date*

_____
_____
_____
_____
_____
_____
_____

*P*rayer Verse _____
_____
_____
_____

M Y • P R A Y E R • P L A N N E R

Photo or Other Visual Reminder

Prayer Request   *Date*

_____

_____

_____

_____

_____

_____

Answer to Prayer   *Date*

_____

_____

_____

_____

_____

_____

*P*rayer Verse _____

_____

_____

<u>Wednesday</u>

*We must move from asking
God to take care of the
things that are breaking our
hearts, to praying about the
things that are breaking
His heart.*

Margaret Gibb

M Y • P R A Y E R • P L A N N E R

Photo or Other Visual Reminder

Prayer Request   *Date*

_____

_____

_____

_____

_____

_____

_____

Answer to Prayer   *Date*

_____

_____

_____

_____

_____

_____

_____

*P*rayer Verse _____

_____

_____

_____

M Y • P R A Y E R • P L A N N E R

Photo or Other Visual Reminder

Prayer Request   *Date*

_____

_____

_____

_____

_____

_____

_____

Answer to Prayer   *Date*

_____

_____

_____

_____

_____

_____

_____

_____

Prayer Verse _____

_____

_____

M Y • P R A Y E R • P L A N N E R

Photo or Other Visual Reminder

Prayer Request   *Date*

_____

_____

_____

_____

_____

_____

_____

Answer to Prayer   *Date*

_____

_____

_____

_____

_____

_____

_____

*P*rayer Verse _____

_____

_____

_____

M Y • P R A Y E R • P L A N N E R

Photo or Other Visual Reminder

Prayer Request   *Date*

_____

_____

_____

_____

_____

_____

_____

Answer to Prayer   *Date*

_____

_____

_____

_____

_____

_____

_____

Prayer Verse _____

_____

_____

_____

MY · PRAYER · PLANNER

Photo or Other Visual Reminder

Prayer Request   *Date*

_____
_____
_____
_____
_____
_____
_____

Answer to Prayer   *Date*

_____
_____
_____
_____
_____
_____
_____

*P*rayer Verse _____
_____
_____
_____

M Y • P R A Y E R • P L A N N E R

Photo or Other Visual Reminder

Prayer Request   *Date*

_____

_____

_____

_____

_____

_____

_____

Answer to Prayer   *Date*

_____

_____

_____

_____

_____

_____

_____

*P*rayer Verse _____

_____

_____

_____

M Y • P R A Y E R • P L A N N E R

Photo or Other Visual Reminder

Prayer Request   *Date*

_____
_____
_____
_____
_____
_____
_____

Answer to Prayer   *Date*

_____
_____
_____
_____
_____
_____
_____

*P*rayer Verse _____
_____
_____
_____

M Y • P R A Y E R • P L A N N E R

Photo or Other Visual Reminder

Prayer Request   *Date*

_____

_____

_____

_____

_____

_____

_____

Answer to Prayer   *Date*

_____

_____

_____

_____

_____

_____

_____

*P*rayer Verse _____

_____

_____

_____

M Y • P R A Y E R • P L A N N E R

Photo or Other Visual Reminder

Prayer Request   *Date*

_____

_____

_____

_____

_____

_____

_____

Answer to Prayer   *Date*

_____

_____

_____

_____

_____

_____

_____

Prayer Verse _____

_____

_____

_____

MY • PRAYER • PLANNER

Photo or Other Visual Reminder

Prayer Request   *Date*

_____

_____

_____

_____

_____

_____

_____

Answer to Prayer   *Date*

_____

_____

_____

_____

_____

_____

_____

Prayer Verse _____

_____

_____

_____

MY • PRAYER • PLANNER

Photo or Other Visual Reminder

Prayer Request   *Date*

_____
_____
_____
_____
_____
_____
_____

Answer to Prayer   *Date*

_____
_____
_____
_____
_____
_____
_____

*P*rayer Verse _____
_____
_____
_____

M Y • P R A Y E R • P L A N N E R

Photo or Other Visual Reminder

Prayer Request   *Date*

_____

_____

_____

_____

_____

_____

_____

_____

Answer to Prayer   *Date*

_____

_____

_____

_____

_____

_____

_____

_____

*P*rayer Verse _____

_____

_____

_____

M Y • P R A Y E R • P L A N N E R

Photo or Other Visual Reminder

Prayer Request   *Date*

_____
_____
_____
_____
_____
_____
_____

Answer to Prayer   *Date*

_____
_____
_____
_____
_____
_____
_____

*P*rayer Verse _____
_____
_____
_____

M Y • P R A Y E R • P L A N N E R

Photo or Other Visual Reminder

Prayer Request   *Date*

_____

_____

_____

_____

_____

_____

_____

Answer to Prayer   *Date*

_____

_____

_____

_____

_____

_____

_____

*P*rayer Verse _____

_____

_____

_____

Thursday

Prayer starts with God.
It is His idea. The desire
to pray is the result of God's
greater desire to talk with
us. He has something to say
when we feel the urge to
prayer.

Lloyd John Ogilvie

M Y • P R A Y E R • P L A N N E R

Photo or Other Visual Reminder

Prayer Request   *Date*

_____

_____

_____

_____

_____

_____

_____

Answer to Prayer   *Date*

_____

_____

_____

_____

_____

_____

_____

*P*rayer Verse _____

_____

_____

_____

M Y • P R A Y E R • P L A N N E R

Photo or Other Visual Reminder

Prayer Request   *Date*

_____

_____

_____

_____

_____

_____

_____

Answer to Prayer   *Date*

_____

_____

_____

_____

_____

_____

_____

Prayer Verse _____

_____

_____

_____

M Y • P R A Y E R • P L A N N E R

Photo or Other Visual Reminder

Prayer Request   *Date*

_____

_____

_____

_____

_____

_____

_____

Answer to Prayer   *Date*

_____

_____

_____

_____

_____

_____

_____

_____

*P*rayer Verse _____

_____

_____

_____

M Y • P R A Y E R • P L A N N E R

Photo or Other Visual Reminder

Prayer Request   *Date*

_____

_____

_____

_____

_____

_____

_____

Answer to Prayer   *Date*

_____

_____

_____

_____

_____

_____

_____

*P*rayer Verse _____

_____

_____

_____

M Y • P R A Y E R • P L A N N E R

Photo or Other Visual Reminder

Prayer Request   *Date*

_____

_____

_____

_____

_____

_____

_____

Answer to Prayer   *Date*

_____

_____

_____

_____

_____

_____

_____

*P*rayer Verse _____

_____

_____

_____

Photo or Other Visual Reminder

Prayer Request   *Date*

_____

_____

_____

_____

_____

_____

_____

Answer to Prayer   *Date*

_____

_____

_____

_____

_____

_____

_____

𝒫rayer Verse _____

_____

_____

_____

MY • PRAYER • PLANNER

Photo or Other Visual Reminder

Prayer Request   *Date*

_____

_____

_____

_____

_____

_____

_____

Answer to Prayer   *Date*

_____

_____

_____

_____

_____

_____

_____

_____

*P*rayer Verse _____

_____

_____

_____

M Y • P R A Y E R • P L A N N E R

Photo or Other Visual Reminder

Prayer Request   *Date*

_____

_____

_____

_____

_____

_____

_____

Answer to Prayer   *Date*

_____

_____

_____

_____

_____

_____

_____

*P*rayer Verse _____

_____

_____

_____

MY · PRAYER · PLANNER

Photo or Other Visual Reminder

Prayer Request   *Date*

_____

_____

_____

_____

_____

_____

_____

Answer to Prayer   *Date*

_____

_____

_____

_____

_____

_____

_____

𝒫rayer Verse _____

_____

_____

_____

Photo or Other Visual Reminder

Prayer Request   *Date*

_____

_____

_____

_____

_____

_____

_____

Answer to Prayer   *Date*

_____

_____

_____

_____

_____

_____

_____

*P*rayer Verse _____

_____

_____

_____

M Y • P R A Y E R • P L A N N E R

Photo or Other Visual Reminder

Prayer Request   *Date*

_____
_____
_____
_____
_____
_____
_____

Answer to Prayer   *Date*

_____
_____
_____
_____
_____
_____
_____

*P*rayer Verse _____
_____
_____
_____

MY • PRAYER • PLANNER

Photo or Other Visual Reminder

Prayer Request   *Date*

_____

_____

_____

_____

_____

_____

_____

Answer to Prayer   *Date*

_____

_____

_____

_____

_____

_____

_____

Prayer Verse _____

_____

_____

_____

M Y • P R A Y E R • P L A N N E R

Photo or Other Visual Reminder

Prayer Request *Date*

_____

_____

_____

_____

_____

_____

_____

Answer to Prayer *Date*

_____

_____

_____

_____

_____

_____

_____

*P*rayer Verse _____

_____

_____

_____

M Y • P R A Y E R • P L A N N E R

Photo or Other Visual Reminder

Prayer Request   *Date*

_____

_____

_____

_____

_____

_____

_____

Answer to Prayer   *Date*

_____

_____

_____

_____

_____

_____

_____

*P*rayer Verse _____

_____

_____

_____

Friday

Beware in your prayers of limiting God, not only by unbelief, but by fancying that you know what He can do. Expect things above all that you ask or think.

Mrs. Charles E. Cowman

MY • PRAYER • PLANNER

Photo or Other Visual Reminder

Prayer Request   *Date*

_____
_____
_____
_____
_____
_____
_____

Answer to Prayer   *Date*

_____
_____
_____
_____
_____
_____
_____

*P*rayer Verse _____
_____
_____
_____

M Y • P R A Y E R • P L A N N E R

Photo or Other Visual Reminder

Prayer Request   *Date*

_____

_____

_____

_____

_____

_____

_____

Answer to Prayer   *Date*

_____

_____

_____

_____

_____

_____

_____

*P*rayer Verse _____

_____

_____

_____

M Y • P R A Y E R • P L A N N E R

Photo or Other Visual Reminder

Prayer Request   *Date*

_____
_____
_____
_____
_____
_____
_____

Answer to Prayer   *Date*

_____
_____
_____
_____
_____
_____
_____

*P*rayer Verse _____
_____
_____
_____

M Y • P R A Y E R • P L A N N E R

Photo or Other Visual Reminder

Prayer Request   *Date*

_____

_____

_____

_____

_____

_____

_____

_____

Answer to Prayer   *Date*

_____

_____

_____

_____

_____

_____

_____

_____

*P*rayer Verse _____

_____

_____

_____

M Y • P R A Y E R • P L A N N E R

Photo or Other Visual Reminder

Prayer Request   *Date*

_____
_____
_____
_____
_____
_____
_____

Answer to Prayer   *Date*

_____
_____
_____
_____
_____
_____
_____

*P*rayer Verse _____
_____
_____

M Y • P R A Y E R • P L A N N E R

Photo or Other Visual Reminder

Prayer Request   *Date*

_____

_____

_____

_____

_____

_____

_____

_____

Answer to Prayer   *Date*

_____

_____

_____

_____

_____

_____

_____

*P*rayer Verse _____

_____

_____

_____

M Y • P R A Y E R • P L A N N E R

Photo or Other Visual Reminder

Prayer Request   *Date*

_____

_____

_____

_____

_____

_____

_____

Answer to Prayer   *Date*

_____

_____

_____

_____

_____

_____

_____

Prayer Verse _____

_____

_____

_____

M Y • P R A Y E R • P L A N N E R

Photo or Other Visual Reminder

Prayer Request

Date

_____
_____
_____
_____
_____
_____
_____

Answer to Prayer

Date

_____
_____
_____
_____
_____
_____
_____

*P*rayer Verse _____

_____
_____

M Y · P R A Y E R · P L A N N E R

Photo or Other Visual Reminder

Prayer Request   *Date*

_____

_____

_____

_____

_____

_____

_____

Answer to Prayer   *Date*

_____

_____

_____

_____

_____

_____

_____

*P*rayer Verse _____

_____

_____

_____

Photo or Other Visual Reminder

Prayer Request   *Date*

_____
_____
_____
_____
_____
_____
_____

Answer to Prayer   *Date*

_____
_____
_____
_____
_____
_____
_____

Prayer Verse _____

_____
_____
_____

M Y • P R A Y E R • P L A N N E R

Photo or Other Visual Reminder

Prayer Request   *Date*

_____
_____
_____
_____
_____
_____
_____

Answer to Prayer   *Date*

_____
_____
_____
_____
_____
_____
_____

*P*rayer Verse _____
_____
_____
_____

M Y • P R A Y E R • P L A N N E R

Photo or Other Visual Reminder

Prayer Request   *Date*

_____

_____

_____

_____

_____

_____

_____

Answer to Prayer   *Date*

_____

_____

_____

_____

_____

_____

_____

*P*rayer Verse _____

_____

_____

_____

MY • PRAYER • PLANNER

Photo or Other Visual Reminder

Prayer Request   *Date*

_____

_____

_____

_____

_____

_____

_____

Answer to Prayer   *Date*

_____

_____

_____

_____

_____

_____

_____

*P*rayer Verse _____

_____

_____

_____

M Y • P R A Y E R • P L A N N E R

Photo or Other Visual Reminder

Prayer Request   *Date*

_____

_____

_____

_____

_____

_____

_____

_____

Answer to Prayer   *Date*

_____

_____

_____

_____

_____

_____

_____

_____

*P*rayer Verse _____

_____

_____

_____

Saturday

Spread out your petition before God, and then say, "Thy will, not mine, be done." The sweetest lesson I have learned in God's school is to let the Lord choose for me.

Dwight L. Moody

M Y • P R A Y E R • P L A N N E R

Photo or Other Visual Reminder

Prayer Request   *Date*

_____

_____

_____

_____

_____

_____

_____

Answer to Prayer   *Date*

_____

_____

_____

_____

_____

_____

_____

*P*rayer Verse _____

_____

_____

_____

M Y • P R A Y E R • P L A N N E R

Photo or Other Visual Reminder

Prayer Request   *Date*

_____

_____

_____

_____

_____

_____

_____

Answer to Prayer   *Date*

_____

_____

_____

_____

_____

_____

_____

*P*rayer Verse _____

_____

_____

_____

MY • PRAYER • PLANNER

Photo or Other Visual Reminder

Prayer Request   *Date*

_____

_____

_____

_____

_____

_____

Answer to Prayer   *Date*

_____

_____

_____

_____

_____

_____

_____

*P*rayer Verse _____

_____

_____

_____

MY • PRAYER • PLANNER

Photo or Other Visual Reminder

Prayer Request   *Date*

_____

_____

_____

_____

_____

_____

_____

Answer to Prayer   *Date*

_____

_____

_____

_____

_____

_____

_____

Prayer Verse _____

_____

_____

_____

MY · PRAYER · PLANNER

Photo or Other Visual Reminder

Prayer Request   *Date*

_____

_____

_____

_____

_____

_____

_____

Answer to Prayer   *Date*

_____

_____

_____

_____

_____

_____

_____

*P*rayer Verse _____

_____

_____

_____

MY • PRAYER • PLANNER

Photo or Other Visual Reminder

Prayer Request   *Date*

_____

_____

_____

_____

_____

_____

_____

Answer to Prayer   *Date*

_____

_____

_____

_____

_____

_____

_____

*P*rayer Verse _____

_____

_____

_____

MY • PRAYER • PLANNER

Photo or Other Visual Reminder

Prayer Request   *Date*

_____

_____

_____

_____

_____

_____

_____

Answer to Prayer   *Date*

_____

_____

_____

_____

_____

_____

_____

*P*rayer Verse _____

_____

_____

_____

Photo or Other Visual Reminder

Prayer Request   Date

_____

_____

_____

_____

_____

_____

_____

Answer to Prayer   Date

_____

_____

_____

_____

_____

_____

_____

*P*rayer Verse _____

_____

_____

_____

MY • PRAYER • PLANNER

Photo or Other Visual Reminder

Prayer Request   *Date*

_____
_____
_____
_____
_____
_____
_____

Answer to Prayer   *Date*

_____
_____
_____
_____
_____
_____
_____

*P*rayer Verse _____
_____
_____
_____

MY • PRAYER • PLANNER

Photo or Other Visual Reminder

Prayer Request   *Date*

_____

_____

_____

_____

_____

_____

_____

Answer to Prayer   *Date*

_____

_____

_____

_____

_____

_____

_____

*P*rayer Verse _____

_____

_____

_____

MY • PRAYER • PLANNER

Photo or Other Visual Reminder

Prayer Request   *Date*

_____
_____
_____
_____
_____
_____
_____

Answer to Prayer   *Date*

_____
_____
_____
_____
_____
_____
_____

*P*rayer Verse _____
_____
_____
_____

M Y • P R A Y E R • P L A N N E R

Photo or Other Visual Reminder

Prayer Request   *Date*

_____
_____
_____
_____
_____
_____
_____

Answer to Prayer   *Date*

_____
_____
_____
_____
_____
_____
_____

*P*rayer Verse _____
_____
_____
_____

MY • PRAYER • PLANNER

Photo or Other Visual Reminder

Prayer Request   *Date*

_____
_____
_____
_____
_____
_____
_____

Answer to Prayer   *Date*

_____
_____
_____
_____
_____
_____
_____

*P*rayer Verse _____
_____
_____
_____

M Y • P R A Y E R • P L A N N E R

Photo or Other Visual Reminder

Prayer Request   *Date*

_____

_____

_____

_____

_____

_____

_____

Answer to Prayer   *Date*

_____

_____

_____

_____

_____

_____

_____

*P*rayer Verse _____

_____

_____

_____

Notes

Notes

Notes

Notes

Notes

Notes

Notes

Notes

Notes

Notes

Notes

Notes